TOGAF™, The Open Group Architecture Framework
A Management Guide

Other publications by Van Haren Publishing on IT Management

Van Haren Publishing specializes in titles on Best Practices, methods and standards within IT and business management. These publications are grouped in two series: ITSM Library (on behalf of itSMF Netherlands) and Best Practice. Current and forthcoming titles include:

ITIL®:

- Foundations of IT Service Management based on ITIL (English, Dutch, French, German, Japanese, Chinese, Danish, Russian, Spanish, Italian, Korean, Brazilian (Portuguese) and Arabic; some editions are also available as a CD-ROM)
- IT Service Management - een samenvatting, 2de druk, A Pocket Guide (Dutch)
- IT Service Management - een leerboek (Dutch)

ISO/IEC 20000:

- ISO/IEC 20000 - A Pocket Guide (English, German, Italian, Japanese and Spanish; Portuguese edition due Autumn 2007)

ISO 27001 and ISO 17799:

- Information Security based on ISO 27001 and ISO 17799 - A Management Guide (English)
- Implementing Information Security based on ISO 27001 and ISO 17799 - A Management Guide (English)

CobiT:

- IT Governance based on CobiT - A Pocket Guide (English, German, Japanese edition available Autumn 2007)

IT Service CMM:

- IT Service CMM - A Pocket Guide (English)

ASL:

- ASL - A Framework for Application Management (English)
- ASL - Application Services Library - A Management Guide (English, Dutch)

BiSL:

- BiSL - A Framework for Business Management and Information Management (Dutch; English edition due 2007)
- BiSL - Business information Services Library- A Management Guide (Dutch; English edition due 2007)

ISPL:

- IT Services Procurement op basis van ISPL (Dutch)
- IT Services Procurement based on ISPL - A Pocket Guide (English)

PRINCE2™:

- Project Management based on PRINCE2™- Edition 2005 (Dutch, English, German)

MSP:

- Programme Management based on MSP (Dutch, English)
- Programme Management based on MSP - A Management Guide (English)

MoR:

- Risk Management based on MoR - A Management Guide (English)

Topics & Management instruments:

- Metrics for IT Service Management (English)
- Six Sigma for IT Management (English)

MOF/MSF:

- MOF - Microsoft Operations Framework, A Pocket Guide (Dutch, English, French, German, Japanese)
- MSF - Microsoft Solutions Framework, A Pocket Guide (English, German)

TOGAF™,
The Open Group
Architecture Framework
A Management Guide

Introducing a comprehensive approach to the design, planning, implementation and governance of an Enterprise Architecture

Chief Author: Tom van Sante

Chief Editor: Hans van den Bent

Colophon

Title:	TOGAF™, The Open Group Architecture Framework
	A Management Guide
Authors:	Tom van Sante (Getronics)
	Janine Kemmeren (Getronics)
	Eelco Rouw (Getronics)
	Dennis Kerssens (Getronics)
	Hans van den Bent (Getronics)
Artwork:	Hans Ringnaida (Getronics)
Editors:	Hans van den Bent (Getronics)
	Jayne Wilkinson
Reviewers:	Chris Greenslade (Clars Limited)
	Cathy Fox (The Open Group)
	Andrew Josey (The Open Group)
Publisher:	Van Haren Publishing (info@vanharen.net)
ISBN (13):	978 90 8753 080 8
Edition:	First edition, first impression, September 2007
Design & layout:	CO2 Premedia, Amersfoort-NL

TRADEMARK NOTICES

Boundaryless Information Flow™ and TOGAF™ are trademarks and The Open Group® is a registered trademark of The Open Group in the United States an other countries.

DISCLAIMER

For further information about Van Haren Publishing, please send an email to info@vanharen.net

Tom van Sante, Janine Kemmeren, Eelco Rouw, Dennis Kerssens and Hans van den Bent have asserted their right to be identified as the Authors of this work under the Copyright, Designs and Patents Act, 1988.

Although every effort has been taken to compose this publication with the utmost care, the Authors, Editors and Publisher cannot accept any liability for damage caused by possible errors and/or incompleteness within this publication. Any mistakes or omissions brought to the attention of the Publisher will be corrected in subsequent editions.

Acknowledgements

Van Haren Publishing gratefully acknowledges The Open Group for permission to reproduce portions of its copyrighted TOGAF^{TM} 2006 Edition, and also for permission to reproduce graphics from The Open Group's Architecture Forum materials.

About the Authors

Tom van Sante

Ir. Tom van Sante started working at Pink Elephant 25 years ago. Pink Elephant eventually became Getronics. Working in a variety of functions he has always operated on the borders between business and IT. He was involved in the introduction and development of ITIL/ASL/BiSL in the Netherlands. He is now responsible for the introduction of TOGAF in Getronics.

Janine Kemmeren

Ing. Janine Kemmeren is Senior Business Consultant and Enterprise Architect with Getronics. Janine has over 12 years of experience in the field of IT and worked in various capacities for a wide variety of projects and customers. For more than five years her focus has been on the field of Enterprise Architecture. Janine is a certified Enterprise Architect and is TOGAF 8 certified.

Eelco Rouw

Dr.Ir. Eelco Rouw started working as an Architect for Getronics after his PhD research at Delft University. During the past three years Eelco has been a Lead IT Architect for several major organizations, including the Port Authority for the largest European sea port and a major European telecom company. He has contributed to many Architecture efforts within Getronics and is TOGAF 8 Certified.

Dennis Kerssens

Drs. Dennis Kerssens is Principal Architect and Business Unit Manager Architecture within Getronics. Dennis has over 17 years of experience in the field of IT and Business Architecture. Dennis is certified Business-ICT-architect and TOGAF 8 certified.

Hans van den Bent

Hans van den Bent MA is Senior Training and Business Consultant with Getronics. Hans has over 18 years of international experience in the field of IT Service Management and

Quality Management. Hans holds all levels of ITIL certification, is TOGAF 8 certified and has co-authored several books in the field of IT Service Management.

About the Reviewers

Chris Greenslade
Chris Greenslade entered the IT profession in 1964 and worked as a consultant, system designer and project manager on a wide variety of projects. He is the proprietor of CLARS Limited, specializing in Enterprise Architecture. After four years of chairing The Open Group 'Architecture Forum', Chris served as an elected Director on The Open Group Governing Board. Now he is Chair of their Supplier Council.

Cathy Fox
Cathy Fox is a Technical Editor at The Open Group. She has been involved in all technical publishing activity at The Open Group over the last 18 years, including TOGAF.

Andrew Josey
Andrew Josey is director of Standards & Certification within The Open Group. He has led the development and operation of many of The Open Group's certification development projects, including industry-wide certification programs for the UNIX system, the Linux Standard Base, Schools Interoperability Framework, The Open Group Architectural Framework, The Open Group Certified IT Architect program, IEEE POSIX, S/MIME Secure Messaging and Secure MIME Gateway. He is currently managing the standards development process for TOGAF.

Table of Contents

Foreword

In only 15 years the role of information in our society has changed dramatically. We are in the middle of an information revolution guided by the need to put the right information in the right people's hands at the right time. Information flows within and between Enterprises as if there are no boundaries between them, save for those needed for security, privacy and governance. It requires infrastructures built on standards and designed to enable individuals, as well as their IT systems, to all work together. Managers have to take decisions on the investments they make in information provision. These decisions have become complex and must be taken more often and faster than ever before.

Enterprise Architecture is a maturing profession that can help management to understand this growing complexity. Enterprise Architecture can reduce complexity by taking a 'city planner' view of the organization, its Information Systems and the infrastructure it runs on. It focuses on building the Enterprise Architecture incrementally, driven by the business needs of the Enterprise, and therefore emerges as a true profession.

TOGAF, The Open Group Architecture Framework, is a fast-growing, worldwide accepted standard that can help organizations build their own Enterprise Architecture in a standardised way. This book explains why this upcoming profession is important, and what TOGAF can do to support you and your Enterprise.

This book explains to management how TOGAF can help in the development of Enterprise Architecture.

Allen Brown, President & Chief Executive Officer
The Open Group

CHAPTER 1

Introduction

*Informed decision-making
comes from a long tradition
of guessing and then blaming
others for inadequate results.*
Scott Adams – the creator of Dilbert

1.1   Why this Management Guide?

This Management Guide explains why decision-making has become complex, and how Enterprise Architecture can support management in decision-making. It also explains the core components of the TOGAF framework from a manager's point of view, and how it can be used.

Organizations have to adapt to the changes around them faster than ever before. In our information-based society this adaptation not only concerns the organization itself, but more and more it also involves their Information Systems. Often, organizations discover that these new demands cannot be resolved with just another new IT solution. Disregarding the existing situation is no longer an option. With most of our Information Systems we are bound to the past even though we have to move towards the future. The fact that, supported by these systems, the flow of information does not stop at organizational boundaries, makes change an especially complex matter. Therefore, the decisions that managers have to make regarding investments in new Information Systems are difficult and full of risk.

Enterprise Architecture supports the decision-making process. Models from different perspectives ('views') within an organization, its Information Systems and its infrastructure are designed to reduce the complexity of the real world. Architecture brings simplicity and overview to the boardroom, to support crucial decisions by producing a destination plan based on different scenarios. It also formalises these decisions and establishes a level of control over their implementation. By developing and adopting Enterprise Architectures, organizations can justify their IT investments and bridge the gap between business and IT. The central concepts of the TOGAF framework are Enterprise Architecture and a process method to build them. A framework like TOGAF is therefore rightfully in the spotlight. TOGAF can be to Enterprise Architecture what ITIL is for Service Management: an open and worldwide accepted framework. By using TOGAF, organizations have a common language, both internally and externally, to describe and discuss Enterprise Architectures and to use this to realise the appropriate IT provision.

1.2   The Open Group: A Vendor-neutral Approach to Architecture

The Open Group is a fast growing and worldwide consortium known for the development of standards and for its range of certification programs

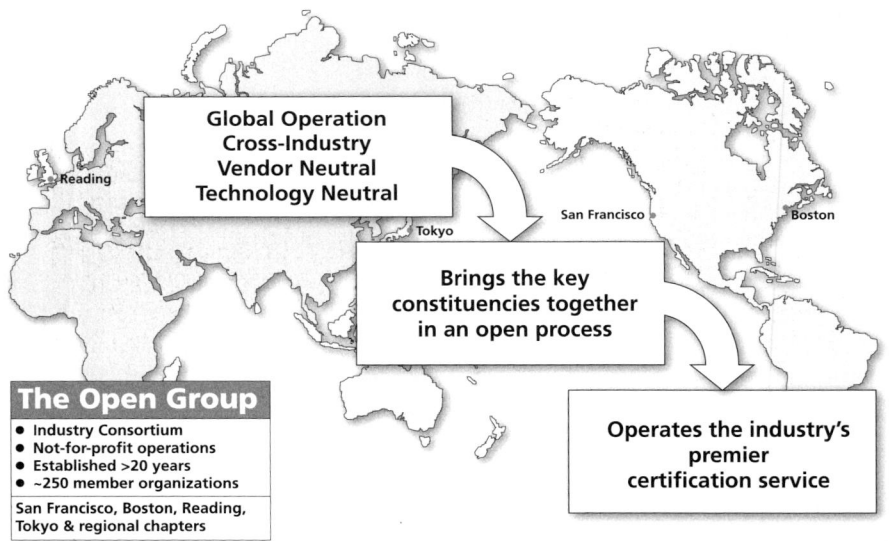

Figure 1.1 *The Open Group promotes global interoperability*

Roughly half of the Open Group membership is from North America, and the rest are equally spread over Europe and the Eastern Pacific. All types of organizations are represented, from a variety of different sectors: from public sector organizations to private companies, from IT companies to banks and industries.

In different forums, the members develop, maintain and support vendor-neutral and technology-neutral open standards for the information society. These standards must support the *Boundaryless Information Flow™*; The Open Group vision of a society where information can flow within and between organizations as if there were no boundaries between them. The results from the workgroups are available for consortium members and, in many cases, for third parties as well. In the Architecture Forum open methods and tools for Enterprise and IT Architectures are developed. The most important and still evolving result of this is The Open Group Architecture Framework (TOGAF™).

Figure 1.2 *The Architecture Forum*

For organizations that want to assess the knowledge and quality of the architects who develop these Architectures, The Open Group has two certification programs, consisting of TOGAF and ITAC (IT Architect Certification) certification. Both the TOGAF framework and the certification scheme for architects support the demand for a common language to enable the production of Enterprise Architectures. TOGAF is an open standard that can help organizations to adapt better and faster to the ever changing demands of their environment.

Apart from the Architecture Forum, The Open Group has a number of other forums dealing with issues that are linked to the development of standards supporting the *Boundaryless Information Flow™*.

1.3   TOGAF

> *TOGAF is the acronym of The Open Group Architecture Framework. It is an Architecture framework which enables you to design, evaluate and build the right Architecture for your organization. TOGAF provides a practical and freely available method to do this. The scope that can be covered by TOGAF includes any organization that delivers products and services in the business and industry domains.*

The Open Group published its first version of TOGAF at the end of 1995. A great milestone was TOGAF 7. TOGAF 7 was based upon the existing Architecture framework for IT Architecture of the American Department of Defence (TAFIM). Added to that were best practices from professional architects and the intellectual property of the participating members. Version 7.1, which is still used by some organizations, had a strong focus on Technology Architecture. Since then the framework has had several reversions. The current version is TOGAF 8.1.1, also known as TOGAF Enterprise Edition. In this edition, the Architecture Development Method (ADM) was quite substantially expanded beyond the Technology Architecture and includes Business Architecture, Information Systems (both data and applications) Architecture, and Technology Architecture. Particularly following the introduction of TOGAF 8.1.1, the number of members and certified architects has grown substantially. Even though The Open Group has a number of streams on different issues, TOGAF, as a part of the Architecture Forum, has attracted interest from a large number of members.

TOGAF is an open framework that can be used by organizations to develop, maintain and employ an Enterprise Architecture. The Open Group provides TOGAF free-of-charge to organizations for their own internal, non-commercial purposes.

The core components of TOGAF are the Architecture Development Method (ADM) and a set of best practices and examples that can help organizations to make their own Enterprise Architecture using the ADM. More precisely the three core components are:
- The *ADM,* which describes in iterative steps the process to develop and maintain an organization's Enterprise Architecture, and how to implement and use this Architecture. It is non-prescriptive about how to build the models that represent the Architecture, but it does tell you what should be done.
- The TOGAF *Resource Base* contains a series of resources; these guidelines, templates and background information are intended to support the ADM.

1994	Requirement	Proof of need
1995	TOGAF Version 1	Proof of concept
1996	TOGAF Version 2	Proof of application
1997	TOGAF Version 3	Relevance to practical architectures (building blocks)
1998	TOGAF Version 4	Enterprise Continuum (TOGAF in context)
1999	TOGAF Version 5	Business Scenarios (architecture requirements)
2000	TOGAF Version 6	Architecture views - IEEE 1471
2001	TOGAF Version 7	Architecture Principles; Compliance Reviews
2002	TOGAF Version 8	Extension to Enterprise Architecture
2003	TOGAF Version 8.1	Requirements Management Governance Maturity Models Skills Framework
2006	TOGAF Version 8.1.1	Technical Corrigendum 1 applied

Figure 1.3 *TOGAF versions since 1994*

- The *Enterprise Continuum,* which is basically an approach to building organization-specific Architectures from reusable components. It starts with using generally available architectural building blocks and it ends with organization-specific solutions in a step-by-step approach.

What makes TOGAF unique is not only its open character. Where other frameworks focus on the Architecture itself and prescribe in detail the different views to be used, TOGAF pays a lot of attention to the organizational commitment as well. It explains how to organise, build and use the right Architecture for your organization. In other words, producing Architecture is not the ultimate goal of the TOGAF framework; making the organization benefit from using the Architecture is.

In the next chapter we describe the general need for Architecture in a complex world.

CHAPTER 2

WHY: Enterprise Architecture

Recognizing the need
is the primary condition
for design.
Charles Eames - designer

In this chapter we will address why developments over past decades have forced managers to make complex decisions and how Enterprise Architectures can help management keep these under control.

2.1 The world keeps changing

> *It is only in the last 15-20 years that we have used the Internet as a means to communicate with each other. Now it is almost impossible to imagine a world without it. No wonder that the transformation from the 20th Century into the 21st Century is often described as our latest revolution.*

Organizations use electronic commerce and participate in networks and supply chains to increase their chances of success. New, fast-growing economies in Asia and Latin America are entering our markets. Globalization is forcing organizations to adapt faster than ever before. Now that information is a major asset of modern economy, the Internet has enlarged the competition enormously. To cope with this, the borders between organizations are beginning to fade. Both inside organizations and between them loosely coupled relations have grown to make organizations capable for change. Organizations that cannot follow this development are being caught up by others that can.

2.1.1 The Boundaryless organization
We have seen organizations consolidate in order to contend with the competition. But now we see successful organizations becoming adaptive collections of business units that co-operate in constantly changing composition, in order to deliver added value to the group. Parts of the organization that do not move fast enough or do not fit in the organizational strategy are sold or sourced elsewhere. If necessary, divisions from other organizations are bought and quickly co-operate with the rest of the organization.

The old structures from which organizations were built can no longer prevail. In the years to come most organizations will become 'boundaryless' and we will see a society emerge where organizations or parts of organizations will be loosely coupled via their information flows. That is when we have reached the information society. As described by Ron Ashkenas ('The Boundary-less Organization'/R.Ashkenas, D.Ulrich, T. Jick and S.Kerr; Jossey-Bass 2002): Twenty-first-century business is in the midst of a social and economic revolution, shifting from rigid to permeable structures and processes and creating something new, namely the "boundaryless organization"

On this image The Open Group has based its vision of Boundaryless Information Flow™. They want to develop, maintain and spread standards to support organizations that have to adapt to these new information flows. The impact of IT investments on day-to-day business is becoming huge. Still managers do not have the time to investigate all of the different alternatives, and often decisions are made based on little or no information at all.

2.1.2   International legislation

International co-operation or international presence for organizations implies that their information flows must take into account international legislation and international standards. For example, the rules in international accounting are laid down in the International Financial Reporting Standards (IFRS). Directors of international concerns represented on the American stock market must adhere to the Sarbanes-Oxley Act (SOX). Alongside this, shareholders want transparency and insight into the ins and outs of the organizations they co-own. The American Government demands from its own organizations that investments in IT assets must be accounted for the 'Clinger & Cohen Act'. Corporate Governance has almost become a matter of public interest. The consequences for IT are obvious. Change will happen more often, is getting more complex, and has to adhere to regulations more than ever before.

2.1.3   Technology push

The enormous change we have seen in our society over the last decade cannot be viewed separately from developments in technology. Even though the expression 24/7 was first used a decade ago, its meaning has changed enormously. At first only a handful of organizations tried to use the Internet as a channel for their day-to-day business. Now, complete industry sectors use the Internet as their only means to interact with customers. The uptake of these developments has grown much faster then we could ever have imagined. The 'network effect[1]' that accomplished this development made the adoption of new technologies move even faster. Today more people and organizations

---

1   Where the number of users of a technology is a prerequisite for its success (ie a fax machine).

worldwide are connected to the Internet – and with faster connections – than we ever thought possible a decade ago.

On the other hand, micro technology has made computer chips grow in capacity but not in size. In combination with wireless technologies, this has produced another explosion of information flows. Many organizations have seen their employees change into multi-device mobile workers who need to be able to work anywhere and at any time. New collaboration tools support these people and process growing amounts of data. Even machines have started to interact with each other by exchanging information without human intervention. While some of us think that these developments can be kept outside the walls of the organization, it is hard to imagine a sector that will not be affected by these changes.

Technology makes things even more complex: without a good structured process to support decision-making and controlling the results, managers will lose control.

2.1.4 Staying in the driving seat

Managers have to make more decisions than ever before. But not only that, more than ever before they will be judged and controlled in doing so.

Scenarios will have to be made and alternative directions planned and decisions recorded in order to be traceable and justified. Within and outside organizations, stakeholders demand a controlled approach to managing the ever growing complexity. To stay in the driving seat managers need governance to maintain control of their organization.

A fundamental process to help understand complexity is needed – in the form of Enterprise Architecture - as a basis for making the right decisions for IT investments.

2.2 Governance

> *In today's business landscape, managers are confronted with increasing amounts of legislation, regulations and shareholder expectations.*

Nowadays, in running a business, it is not only important to have a robust vision, a clear strategy and realistic planning, but also the evidence that the company is able to pursue its stated business goals in a controlled and predictable way. The manager should be in the driver's seat.

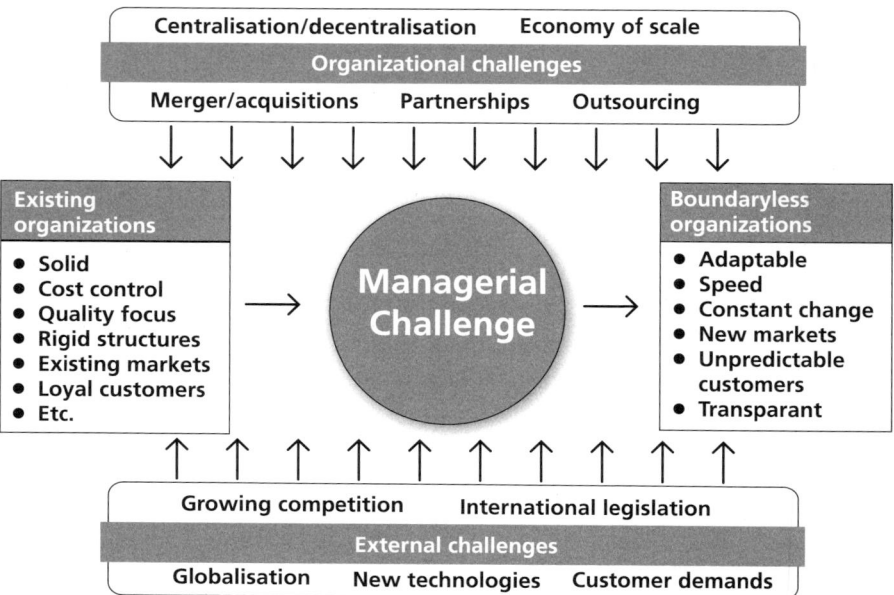

Figure 2.1 *Challenges for today's management*

2.2.1   What is Governance

After the Enron affair, 'compliance' has become a standard in the vocabulary of most managers. The resulting regulations, such as the Sarbanes Oxley Act (SOX), confront managers with their responsibility to control and manage (financial) risks effectively.

Furthermore, the business landscape is becoming more aggressive and competitive. Companies that are able to adapt, form alliances and direct their business to stay ahead of the competition are the sole survivors. Information technology has become a firm prerequisite for a successful business. The possibilities offered by IT, to share and exchange knowledge, have rapidly increased the complexity of most businesses.

Running a business nowadays requires strong entrepreneurial and analytical skills to make the right decisions at the right time. Translated to most businesses this requires a strong vision and a framework of rules, regulations and procedures enabling management to make effective decisions based on arguments instead of assumptions and 'gut feeling'. The sum of all regulations, procedures, processes and responsibilities is referred to as 'governance'.

Governance is a diffuse and somewhat hyped term, with multiple viewpoints and interpretations mainly dependent upon who you are speaking to. However, most people agree that governance is all about controlling the day-to-day business of your organization and its development. It comprises a set of rules and procedures to control and maintain risks and enable organizations to fulfil the expectations of its stake- and shareholders. Governance can be seen on different levels with differing scopes, such as IT Governance, Financial Governance, Corporate Governance or Enterprise Governance. Scopes can range from single processes to departments or complete organizations, either on the strategic, tactical or operational level.

An important aspect of governance is to provide strategic management with a 'company dashboard'. The dashboard provides management with information regarding the key performance indicators such as production throughput, costs, employee efficiency, etc.

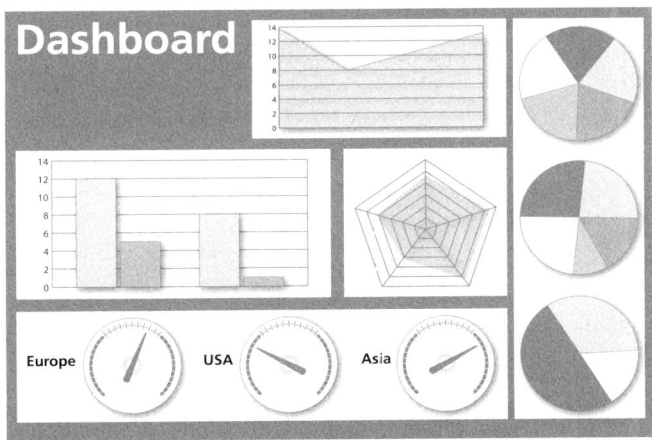

Figure 2.2 *Company Dashboard*

Developing a suitable governance structure within an organization helps to overcome cumbersome, diffuse and slow decision-making processes, while reducing risks. Identifying the various responsibilities and information required for decisions vastly reduces the complexity of managing a business.

Implementing and enabling governance throughout the organization provides a strong foundation for a robust and successful business, able to cope with the increasing amounts of legislation and shareholder demands.

2.2.2   How can governance be achieved

For most organizations the implementation of governance is a complex and difficult challenge, as it impacts the political landscape of the organization and its surrounding environment. Thinking about the processes, procedures, responsibilities and information required for decision-making can be quite daunting. It is not unlikely that the rationale behind earlier business decisions is severely lacking, something that becomes clear when implementing a suitable governance structure.

For the actual implementation of governance structures different frameworks exist that can assist businesses in defining the processes and responsibilities. Examples of such best practices include CoBiT (IT Governance) and Six Sigma (Corporate Governance). These frameworks provide blueprints for the various processes needed for effective control, and help businesses to develop their own governance structures.

As the business changes continuously, most governance processes have a cyclical nature which roughly corresponds to the business planning and strategy cycles.

A famous example of a simple governance process is the Deming Cycle. This process enables businesses to set their goals, implement the required procedures, and to monitor and develop their business.

Figure 2.3 *The Deming Quality Cycle*

Two key ingredients for a successful implementation of governance are:
*   **an organizational structure**, clearly defining stakeholders and their role in the governance processes

- **an overview of the business**, clearly defining dependencies, relationships and requirements

Most available frameworks contain definitions of the organizational structure. Simple instruments such as RACI tables (Responsible, Accountable, Consulted and Informed) enable clear definitions for the different roles of stakeholders.
Having all the processes and organizational structures for governance in place may give your business high marks with many accounting firms, but it will not help you to achieve your business goals. As stated earlier, it is important to have a clear vision and strategy.

2.2.3   Why use Architecture

For a strategy to work, it is necessary to have an insight into the current mode of operation (as-is, baseline, IST) and the desired state of the business (to-be, target, SOLL). The planning horizon of the desired state depends entirely on the business, ranging from one year (for rapidly changing businesses) to several years.
In order to control and direct the business it is important to have knowledge of the components, structures and systems that constitute the business, and support the corporate vision for the current state, and the desired state in the future. The corporate strategy and vision should be translated into a set of blueprints for the business, representing the current and the desired state. Developing both blueprints simultaneously enables the creation of corporate roadmaps.

These blueprints assist decision-makers by providing them with the right information from different viewpoints, such as cost, capacity, security, efficiency, etc. In fact, the blueprint provides a representation of the business and its surrounding environment.

Developing and maintaining blueprints requires strong analytical skills and is a complex task. Therefore, most decision-makers should be assisted by *Trusted Advisors* who are able to counsel them based on rational arguments and a comprehensive knowledge of the business and its various aspects.
The corporate architect should be regarded as the embodiment of an important, trusted advisor, as they have the tools and skills to determine the impact and risks of business decision-making. The process of defining these business blueprints is referred to as *architecting* and the resulting blueprints are mostly referred to as *Architecture*.

Traditionally, Architecture is a discipline surrounded by miscommunication and inflated expectations. When implemented properly it can provide the relevant information to enable decision-makers to make the right business decisions. A blueprint supplies decision-makers with rational arguments and facilitates 'what if?' scenarios.

Essentially, Architecture helps and supports the decision process, it formalizes the decisions taken and it controls the evolution of the IT. To be more precise, Architecture provides businesses with three key ingredients for decision-making:

- **A common framework and language;** Architecture provides a common framework, a set of definitions and language, which can be used throughout the organization to facilitate interdisciplinary communication.
- **Alignment through insight**; Architecture provides an overview of the business and its environment, it enables the identification of relations between organization, technology and processes on different levels; this varies from a corporate strategy to the resulting guidelines that should be followed for the design of a new Information System or business process.
- **Control through insight;** the Architecture *management process* enables businesses to monitor and control business developments throughout the lifecycle, ranging from the conception of a new venture/business idea, through the implementation and finally to control/evolution.

Architecture provides the key ingredients to implement and aid governance in organizations and enable organizations to effectively implement and control their vision and corporate strategy.

2.3 Architecture

Architecture *(Noun)*
The fundamental organization of a system, embodied in its components, their relationships to each other and the environment, and the principles governing its design and evolution.[2]

2.3.1 What is Architecture?
The word Architecture is not coincidental, but is deliberately linked to the world of construction. But that does not make it an exact science. When we look at famous buildings built in the ages before us we sometimes express our admiration for the

---

2   ANSI/IEEE Std 1471-2000, Recommended Practice for Architectural Description of Software-Intensive Systems.

Architecture achieved. But this is just as misleading as it is in IT Architecture. We admire the end result but forget about the complex processes that must have preceded it. The creator of the technical models in the architects' office often considers himself to be the architect of the design, since he is the one who makes all the blueprints of the future building. But it is the architect who relates the client's requirements to the building regulations, and who works out the technological possibilities. And with these blueprints the architect instructs and controls the builder so that the design will lead to a useful building. This is probably the most important aspect of the expression 'Architecture'.

It is not unexpected that there are many definitions of IT Architecture, but in principle they have much in common. The most commonly used is from the American National Standards Institute (ANSI / IEEE Std 1471-2000).

The most common concepts are:
- a **framework** for ordering concepts and assets; for instance, the Zachman framework identifies six viewpoints related to specific stakeholders and for each viewpoint six aspects to describe the Architecture; that is, why, what, who, where, when and how.
- a **method** to give structure to the objects of interest; Architecture can be defined by the invention, creation and management of Architectures, as well as to supervise the realization and maintenance of the final system according to the Architecture; the Architecture Development Method (ADM), as part of TOGAF, is an example of such a method; this ADM is explained in Chapter Four
- a collection of **principles** to restrict the solutions; these principles are most often written down in laws or regulations
- a **blueprint** of the organization with all its parts and their interrelations
- a **design** of the construction of a single solution, such as a single software system

If management wants to use Architecture in the most complete manner, all of these concepts are needed.

The fact that today's organizations depend more and more on information makes the need for Business IT alignment a popular issue. Future business directions and IT decisions need to be based on the same business goals in order to be in line with each other. Therefore, apart from the different concepts that address the notion of Architecture, a distinction can be made between types of Architectures. The Open Group uses a concept of Architecture called the Enterprise Architecture. Four kinds of Architectures have been defined as part of the Enterprise Architecture:
- Business Architecture
- Data Architecture

- Applications Architecture
- Technology Architecture

An Enterprise in the concept of Enterprise Architecture can be any collection of organizations that has a common set of goals. More and more this means that the Enterprise can be the organization and its partners.

Architectures reveal the structure and the underlying principles of a company and its IT, its present state well as its future state. This is indispensable for keeping a control of the company and for enabling controlled migrations within the company. But Architecture is more than that. We also refer to it as the process that the organization uses to formalize the current and future structure. Managers act as constituents to Architects who guide this process.

Because of the speed of change and the growing competition, standardization and re-use are basic principles in modern business; like building different houses for different users or occupants, and using prefab elements in order to work quickly and to compete with the competition. Architecture helps to identify opportunities in standardizing parts of the business or IT, improving the interaction between these parts, and reducing cost or risks by making more re-use of existing Architectures or implementations.

Like future users of a building, organizations also have multiple users of future IT systems. They all have their own ideas of what the future state should be, and the people that build the future state all need their own instructions to reach the desired result. Architecture and Architectures are needed to keep all those who are involved informed and committed to reach the common goals. In order to do this they explain the transformations by using 'views' so that everyone understands the consequences involved related to their own 'viewpoint'. In other words, the future user of a kitchen is not really interested in the wiring needed to make the oven work and equally, the electrician is not interested in what can be cooked in it. In the end, it is the architect who can link these two together.

2.3.2   What is an Architect?

Like the architect of a building is an intermediary between the client's wishes, the regulatory possibilities, the builder's capabilities and the solution in the end, the IT Architect performs a similar role. It is not so much the plans and designs that make his work useful, it is more the way in which he uses these designs to consolidate and condense the decisions of all those involved, in such a way as to ensure that everyone can co-operate to make the desired state. A successful architect manages this process to the full benefit of his management. We all have ideas and visions of the architect's role in the building process and therefore we can imagine the IT Architect's role in the business world.

2.3.3   How to do Architecture

Managers can benefit from the use of Architecture when managing the company or its IT. It helps to gain control over the implementation of the company's aims throughout all the structures of business and IT in the company. Adding Architecture to the agenda of the Board will suggest that new aspects are introduced into the decision-making process; managing the company to use Architecture to its benefit will be an extra task to fulfill.

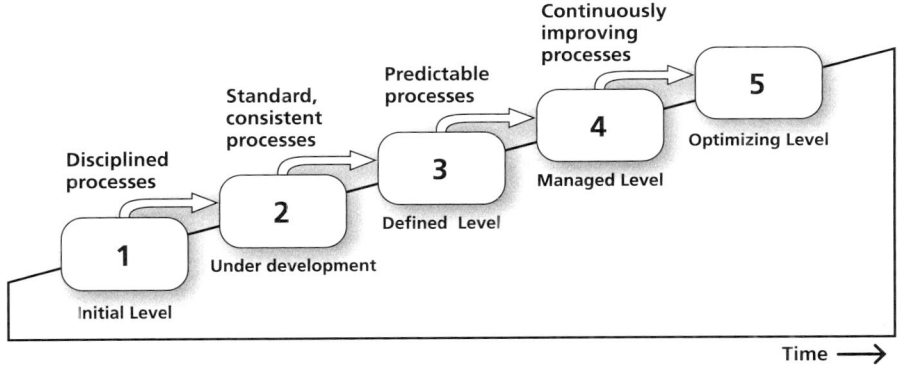

Figure 2.4 *Architecture Capability Maturity Model*

Introducing Architecture into the organization, in a controlled way and with maximum commitment from the people involved, is not normally an overnight process. Organizations normally only slowly mature in their Architecture approach. Like it can be seen in the Capability Maturity Model (CMM) this maturing process follows standard steps:

- In the first stage (initial), awareness is created among the stakeholders about the function that Architecture can have within the company.
- In the second stage (under development), activities concerning Architecture are assigned to persons within the company.
- In the third stage (defined), the processes concerning Architecture are well defined and repeatable.
- In the fourth stage (managed), the company is focusing on the Architecture deliverables instead of the Architecture process.

- And finally, in the fifth stage (optimizing), the company focusses on the continuous improvement of the architectural approach. Architecture is no longer a separate activity in relation to issues like business planning, or IT development and deployment. It has become an integral aspect of the total governance of the company and is embedded in the business.

In this last stage, many aspects are considered with their mutual interdependencies. For instance, cost is taken into account. Politics are considered:

- Who are the stakeholders and what are their roles and influences within the decision-making process?
- On what terms will the final solution be acceptable for the people involved in the system?
- What are the capabilities of the organization, such as the available competencies or the ability to change?

All of these aspects have their own trade-offs. Architecture is all about searching for the best structures to fit the needs of all the stakeholders, taking all trade-offs into account.

2.3.4   Why choose TOGAF

Because there are different methods and frameworks available, the company should select (and probably customize) the one that fits best to the interests of the organization. As companies become more and more interlinked, it becomes necessary to adopt a common vocabulary, method and framework, in order to streamline the communication about Architecture and to create Architectures that fit together, not only within the organizations, but also among them. In this way, value chains of conglomerates of interlinked companies can adopt quickly, but still independently from one another, and operate more efficiently and effectively.

TOGAF aims to be such an open standard. It is widely accepted and growing in popularity. It is based on many good practices in different industries, and it is available for any company. In essence, TOGAF gives guidance for the Architecture process.

In TOGAF, the expression *Architecture* has two meanings, depending upon the context in which it is being used:
- a formal description of a system, or a detailed plan of the system at component level to guide its implementation
- the structure of components, their inter-relationships, and the principles and guidelines governing their design and evolution over time

In this way, TOGAF embraces, but does not strictly adhere to, ANSI/IEEE Std 1471-2000 terminology. TOGAF endeavours to strike a balance between promoting the concepts and terminology of ANSI/IEEE Std 1471-2000, and retaining other commonly accepted terminology that is familiar to the majority of TOGAF users.

TOGAF distinguishes itself from other major Architecture models with its Architecture Development Method (ADM), a process approach to the development of Architectures. Another part of the TOGAF Architecture-approach is to select the appropriate standards and reusable prefabricated Architectures, whilst also keeping control over the deliverables of the architecting process. This will enable the company to create an 'Architecture knowledge base', that is, a 'virtual repository' of all the Architecture assets, models, patterns, Architecture descriptions, etc. For this knowledge base TOGAF introduces the concept of the Enterprise Continuum and provides a Resource Base with reusable standards and pre-fabricated Architectures.

Because TOGAF is a generic framework, it can be customized and optimized for use in your own organization. TOGAF itself gives hints on how to customize and extend your complete Architecture 'toolbox', with references to Architecture frameworks, TOGAF-supporting tools, etc.

CHAPTER 3

WHAT: Understanding the TOGAF Model

*"We can't solve problems by
using the same kind of thinking
we used when we created them."*
Albert Einstein

In this chapter the TOGAF Model is explained, in order to create a better understanding of the core components of TOGAF and how they can be used.

The *Architecture Development Method (ADM)* will be discussed phase by phase, because it is the key component of TOGAF. The *Enterprise Continuum*, which supports the ADM, will be described including the rationale behind it. Finally, an outline of the *Resource Base* is given.

3.1 TOGAF Core Components

The ADM is a process for developing an Enterprise Architecture in a way that will secure the involvement and commitment of all stakeholders on different levels within the organization. After this, the different Architectures are built in a step-by-step approach, and constantly linked to the business needs. By doing this, the Architecture will better match the needs of the organization and subsequently, the solutions that are built will better match the chosen Architecture. It will be easier to predict the success of future IT solutions.

To support the ADM process the Enterprise Continuum is used; a 'virtual repository' of all the Architecture assets that the organization needs. It provides general reference models or organization-specific building blocks, so you never start with a blank sheet of paper. The third element of TOGAF is the Resource Base: a set of documents including guidelines, whitepapers, templates and other background information.

The three main parts of TOGAF: ADM, Enterprise Continuum and Resource Base, are explained in more detail in the following sections.

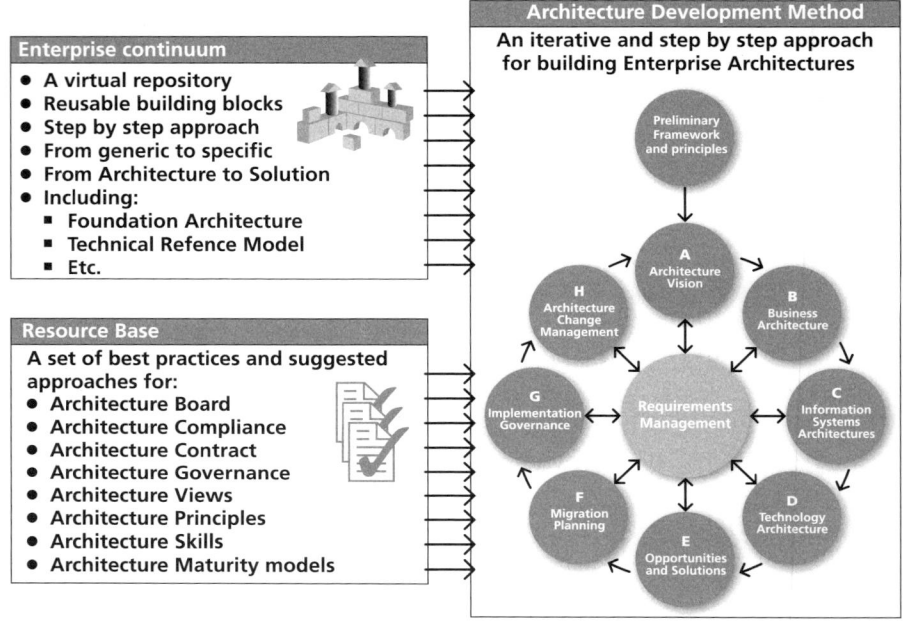

Figure 3.1 *TOGAF Components*

3.2   The Architecture Development Method

The Architecture Development Method (ADM) is the key to TOGAF; it is a reliable, proven process model that describes how to implement Architecture in your organization.

Even though its representation suggests a step-by-step process model, it is often referred to as an iterative approach. During the ADM, different Architecture Views are produced, and used to communicate with all those involved, in order to develop the right solutions.

The ADM can be tailored to meet the specific needs of an organization. Some of the phases might be unnecessary, depending on the maturity of the Architecture discipline in the organization. Some procedures may need to be modified to comply with Corporate Governance rules, to maximize the benefits from existing processes or to deal with Enterprise specific situations. Maybe even some new procedures will need to be added. All this may be required to make sure that the processes interact optimally with project planning and management methods, and with processes such as risk analysis, authorization of expenditure, measuring and reporting of business performance and procurement.

The ADM is an iterative process cycle, with sub stages that may be iterative too. During each round of the ADM cycle, an organization needs to decide on the scope that needs to be covered, and on the level of detail that has to be defined. Decisions also have to be made as to the length of the time horizon and the architectural assets that will be used from the Enterprise Continuum. The main guideline for these decisions is to focus on what creates value to the Enterprise, and to select scope and time horizons accordingly. Future iterations will build on what is built in the present, adding greater width and depth to the projected output. The longer an organization uses TOGAF to build and use Enterprise Architecture, the greater the results will be.

3.2.1   The Preliminary Phase: Framework & Principles

The importance of the Preliminary Phase is to define HOW Architecture will be implemented in a specific organization. Deciding what *framework* to use and to what detail, defining the *Architecture Principles* and establishing the *governance* are the three main aspects of this phase.

In this phase, it is important to answer questions such as:

- What business goals do we have?
- To what detail do we have to describe our Architecture in order to benefit from it?

Before the actual Architecture work begins, the organization must decide what the principles will be for re-use. The framework will also explain how re-use is affected. All these questions and more must be answered and accepted by the organization. Another function of the Preliminary Phase is to review the components of the framework to check that they are applicable. These should then be tailored, as explained earlier, to the circumstances of the individual Enterprise, producing an 'Enterprise-specific' ADM.

The first important step in this phase is commitment to the architectural approach. This is to ensure that everyone involved or benefiting from the project is committed to the success of the architectural process. Organizations that plan to use Enterprise Architecture to support and control their future decisions must be aware that commitment is needed

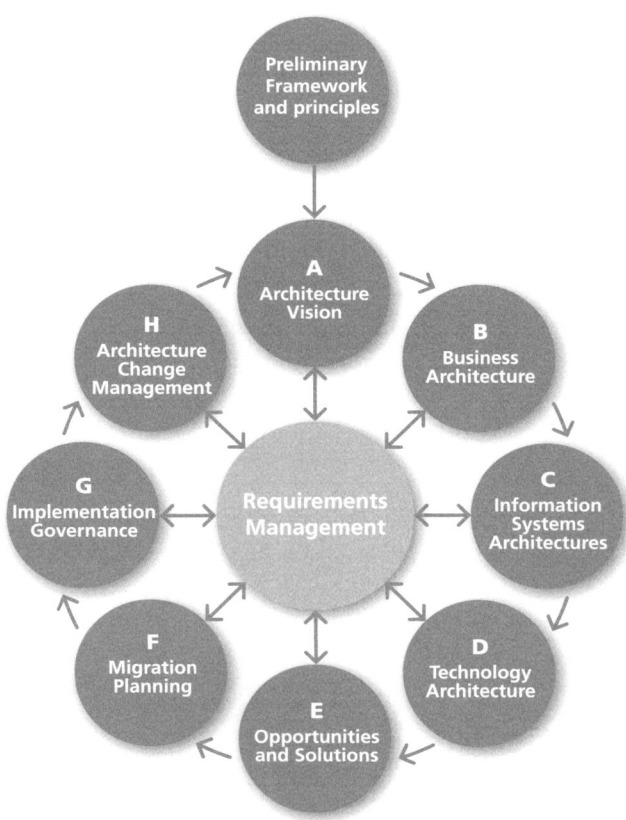

Figure 3.2 *Phases of the Architecture Development Method (ADM)*

at every level of the organization in order to get maximum benefit. Therefore, in this phase it is necessary to identify the resistance points from all stakeholders and to ensure that they are dealt with. Using an existing or newly developed *IT Governance Strategy*, the governance for the Architecture Development Process can be established. With this, the focus on what can be achieved with Enterprise Architecture is ensured.

The outputs of this phase, the *Framework Definition*, the *Architecture Principles*, and the *Business Principles*, *Business Goals* and *Business Drivers* are used to start Phase A, creating the Architecture Vision.

3.2.2   Phase A: Architecture Vision

This phase is about proper *recognition and endorsement* by corporate management, and support and commitment from management for the work to be undertaken in this phase of the ADM cycle. Phase A also defines what is inside and what is outside of the *scope* of the Architecture effort, and what the *constraints* are that must be dealt with in the following phases. Scoping decisions need to be made, based on a practical assessment of available resources and competencies, and on the value that can be realistically expected to accrue from the Architecture work. Phase A and the ADM cycle begin with an Architecture Project Initiation Document called a *Request for Architecture Work*.

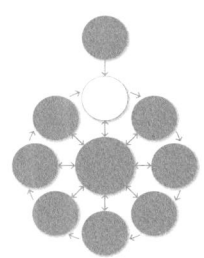

Creating the *Architecture Vision* is the most important activity in this phase, because the Architecture Vision is essentially the architect's 'elevator pitch', used to sell the benefits of the proposed development to the decision-makers within the Enterprise. The goal is to articulate an Architecture Vision that clarifies the purpose of the Architecture effort, and verifies, or records, the documented business strategy and goals, so that everyone involved can agree on them. In this phase, the Baseline Architecture and the Target Architecture are described in a general way.

The final step in Phase A is to produce the Statement of Architecture Work based on the Request for Architecture Work. Appropriate governance procedures are described here to facilitate a secure formal approval process. Business scenarios are used to review the business vision, strategy and drivers. Then a set of business requirements is generated for the future Enterprise. From this the conceptual Enterprise Architecture is created and the first-cut 'drawings and designs' are produced, allowing the business to see what the Enterprise will look like in its targeted state. In this way we deliver the Architecture Vision including Baseline and Target Architectures for the Business, Data, Applications and Technology domains.

The approved *Statement of Architecture Work* is taken to the next phase as a formal assignment. The Architecture Principles, Architecture Vision and Enterprise Continuum will be used as a starting point for execution during the next phase.

3.2.3   Phase B: Business Architecture

The next phases B, C and D focus on developing the individual Architecture Specifications that make up the whole Enterprise Architecture. These phases create different views on the Enterprise Architecture, looking at each stakeholder's area of interest. While the main flow of decision-making is from B to C and from C to D, these are iterative phases that cycle until the final versions of each are achieved and signed off by the sponsor and stakeholders.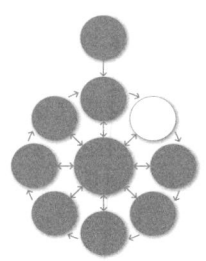

Phase B is aimed at verifying and documenting the Enterprise mission, vision, strategy and goals (they may also be documented as part of some wider business strategy or Enterprise planning activity). The Business Architecture is often used to demonstrate the business value of Technology Architecture work to key stakeholders, and the return on investment (ROI) to those stakeholders from supporting and participating in these activities. Another key objective is to re-use existing material as much as possible. In architecturally mature environments, there are existing Architecture Definitions, which have been maintained since the last Architecture Development Cycle; these can be used as a starting point, and updated if necessary.

To complete the Business Architecture we use the selected standards and fully document each Architecture Building Block. The result of this is a Target Business Architecture that describes the product and/or service strategy, and the organizational, functional, process, information and geographic aspects of the business environment, all based on the business principles, the business goals and the strategic drivers.

Finally, a Gap Analysis is performed, and a report is produced, with the gap matrix and the identified building blocks to be carried over. Building blocks are classified as changed or unchanged, eliminated or new. The results and products of this phase will be handed over to the next phase as an input for developing the Information Systems Architecture.

3.2.4   Phase C: Information Systems Architectures

Phase C creates the Information Systems Architectures that supports the Business Architecture. In this phase we aim to translate the requirements that have led to the Business Architecture into consequences for the Data and the Applications Architecture. Phase C thus involves a combination of Data and Applications Architecture depending on the scope, and the business goals and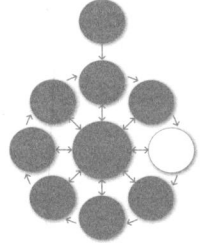

principles. An organization can start with the Data Architecture or with the Applications Architecture to develop the Information Systems Architecture.

For each viewpoint one or more Architecture Models are created, using a selected tool or method. It is important to ensure that all stakeholder concerns are covered in the generated views. The application systems are related to business functions in the Business Architecture.

A formal checkpoint review is conducted with the stakeholders of the Architecture Models and building blocks. This is followed by a review of the qualitative criteria, providing as many measurable criteria as possible. These criteria can be used to specify required service levels to serve as input for formal Service Level Agreements.

For both domains a checkpoint and impact analysis is conducted:
* Is the original motivation for the Architecture project still valid?
* Is the Statement of Architecture Work still valid compared to the Data and Applications Architecture?

If necessary, the Business Architecture may need changes in response to the change in the Data and Applications Architecture. And finally, any constraints that may exist on the Technology Architecture need to be identified. As a last step in this phase, a Gap Analysis is performed and a report is created based on this analysis.

3.2.5   Phase D: Technology Architecture

In Phase D the Technology Architecture that will be the foundation for the target IT infrastructure is created. The Applications and Data Architectures are translated into a Technology Architecture, taking all aspects from the Business Architecture into account. The Architectures can be used as procurement guidelines to govern the future growth and development of the organization's IT infrastructure. In this step there is a transition from product documentation to a service-oriented description. Relevant parts of the existing Architecture (using the scope definition established 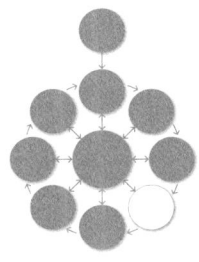 in Phase A) are captured as candidates for reusable building blocks. The existing Architecture is assessed against the Business Architecture, identifying the key inhibitors and the opportunities for re-use. Finally, the existing Architecture assessment ends with the capture of implied or explicit Architecture Principles that should be used in this Architecture project.

The steps in the Technology Architecture phase are the same as those followed in the Information Systems Architecture phase. As with the first step in that phase, a Baseline Architecture Description is created to provide a common starting point. Then different Architecture Reference Models, viewpoints and tools are considered to ensure that all requirements from all stakeholders are covered.

The Target Architecture can now be fully specified by documenting all interfaces for Technology Architecture each building block and selecting standards for each interface of the Architecture Building Blocks, re-using as much as possible from the Technical Reference Model. After conducting a Gap Analysis to identify any missing functionality, we have developed a Technological Architecture that will form the basis for implementation in the next phases.

3.2.6   Phase E: Opportunities and Solutions

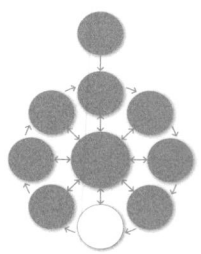

Phase E identifies the parameters of change, the major phases along the way, and the top-level projects to move from the current environment to the target environment. The output of Phase E is the basis of the Implementation Plan for the Target Architecture. This phase also attempts to identify new business opportunities arising from the Architecture work in previous phases. Sometimes, the process of identifying implementation opportunities allows the business to identify new applications. This can be the case when making build-versus-buy-versus-re-use decisions or assessing the dependencies, costs and benefits of the various projects, and while planning the overall implementation and migration strategy.

Phase E is the first phase which is directly concerned with implementation. The task is to identify the major work packages or projects to be undertaken.

3.2.7   Phase F: Migration Planning

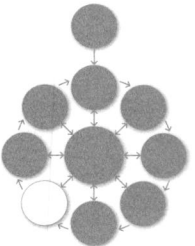

The objective of Phase F is to sort the various implementation projects that were selected in the previous phase by priority. There are some important questions that need to be asked before moving on to migration:

- What are the implications of the project(s)?
- What are the dependencies between them?
- What products are needed?
- What are the costs and benefits?
- What are the resource requirements?

Many things affect the answers to these questions, including the current and future Architectures or the size of the organization and its complexity. But also the value of technology to the core functions of the organization. It is important to consider the asset value of the current systems, and the level of risk associated with changing the solution and/or the supplier.

In many cases, a change is too complex and has too much impact on the organization to be implemented in a single phase. A number of technical issues must be considered when moving on to migration of the environment. Very often these are associated with the means of introducing change to operational systems, giving much concern for operational systems and ongoing business. Issues requiring special attention may include parallel operations, choices of proceeding with phased migration by subsystem or by function, and the impact of geographical separation on migration. The decisions resulting from this should be incorporated in the Implementation Plan.

Phase F delivers an implementation with a time-lined implementation roadmap, including a draft of an Architecture Implementation contract.

3.2.8 Phase G: Implementation Governance
In this phase all the information for successful management of the various implementation projects is brought together. There will be a lot of co-operation with other professions in the organization, in order to get the changes performed in a controlled way. Phase G establishes the connection between Architecture and the implementation organization. This phase will control the ultimate deliverable: the implemented Architecture-compliant system(s).

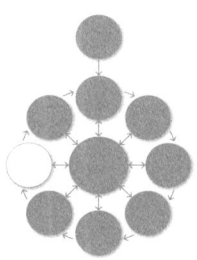

For each implementation project recommendations are formulated and followed by the construction of an Architecture Contract, in order to govern the overall implementation and deployment process. Appropriate governance functions are performed while the system is being implemented and deployed. This is done with the objective of ensuring conformance with the defined Architecture.

3.2.9 Phase H: Architecture Change Management
The goal of the Architecture Change Management phase is to ensure that changes to the Architecture are managed and to establish an implemented Enterprise Architecture that is dynamic. This means an Architecture that has the flexibility to evolve rapidly in response to changes in the technology and business environment.

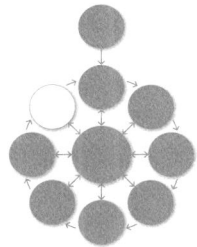

The Change Management process will determine the circumstances under which the Enterprise Architecture, or parts of it, should change after implementation, and the process by which this is controlled.

The Architecture Change Management process is very closely related to the Architecture Governance processes in the Enterprise. This process is also involved with the management of the Architecture Contract between the Architecture function and the business users of the Enterprise. In Phase H it is critical that the governance body establishes criteria to judge whether a change request warrants just an Architecture update or whether it justifies starting a new cycle of the Architecture Development Method (ADM). It is especially important to avoid 'creeping elegance', and the governance body must continue to look for changes that relate directly to business value.

3.2.10 Requirements Management

Requirements Management is not a real phase, but the linchpin between phases with respect to requirements. As indicated by the 'Requirements Management' circle at the centre of the ADM graphic, the ADM is continuously driven by the Requirements Management process. The requirements that are managed are not a static set, but are part of a dynamic process, whereby requirements for Enterprise Architecture and subsequent changes to those requirements, are identified, stored and fed into and out of the relevant ADM phases.

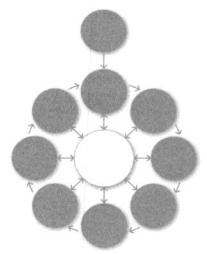

The ability to deal with changes in requirements is crucial. Architecture is an activity that, by its very nature, deals with uncertainty and change. There is a *grey area* between stakeholders' ambitions and what can be specified and engineered as a solution. In practice, Architecture requirements are therefore invariably subject to change. Moreover, Architecture often deals with drivers and constraints, many of which, by their very nature, are beyond the control of the Enterprise (changing market conditions, new legislation, etc.), and which can produce changes in requirements in an unforeseen manner.

3.3 The Enterprise Continuum

> *The Enterprise Continuum is a set of reusable components: a virtual repository. It contains Architecture assets, models, patterns, Architecture descriptions, business descriptions, building blocks and other Architecture products.*

The components of the Enterprise Continuum can be drawn from within the Enterprise or from the IT industry at large. They are the products that the Enterprise considers to be available for the development of Architectures for the Enterprise. The Enterprise Continuum is an important aid to communication and understanding. Architectures are specific to the context in which they are used, and therefore a consistent language is needed to communicate effectively the differences between Architectures. The Continuum provides that consistent language. Knowing 'where in the continuum you are', avoids people talking at cross purposes. It helps to organize reusable Architecture and solution assets.

The Enterprise Continuum is the combination of the two concepts: *Architecture Continuum* and *Solutions Continuum*.

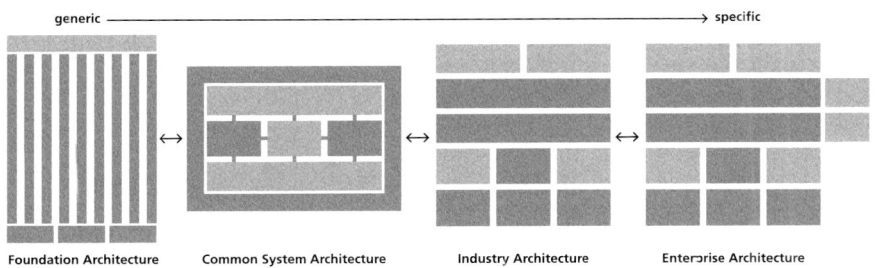

Figure 3.3 *The Architecture Continuum*

The Architecture Continuum provides a consistent way to define and understand the generic rules, representations and relationships in an Information System. It offers a consistent way to understand the Architectures and their components. The Architecture Continuum classifies reusable Architecture Assets, and in this it is directly supported by the Solutions Continuum. The Architecture Continuum stretches from the most general Foundation Architecture on the left, to the most specific Architecture, the Enterprise Architecture, on the right. The Foundation Architecture consists of the

Technical Reference Model (TRM) and the Standards Information Base (SIB), both described in more detail in the next section. The Foundation Architecture describes the fundamental Architecture upon which more specific Architectures can be based. The ADM explains how to develop an Enterprise-specific Architecture based on the Foundation Architecture.

The Solutions Continuum provides a consistent way to describe and understand the implementation of the Architecture Continuum. It provides a way to understand the different products, systems, services and solutions. It defines what is available in the organization and its environment as reusable building blocks and addresses the commonalities and differences among the products, systems and services of implemented systems. Solution Architectures are populated with functionality components. The solutions represent the implementation of the Architectures and are a practical realization of the Conceptual Architecture.

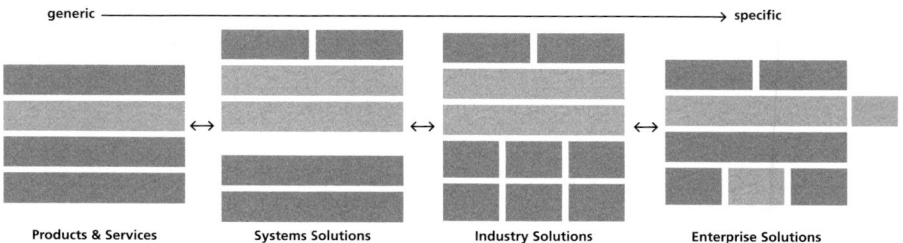

Figure 3.4 *The Solutions Continuum*

Together, the Architecture Continuum and the Solutions Continuum form the Enterprise Continuum.

The relationship between the Architecture Continuum and the Solutions Continuum is one of guidance, direction and support. A similar relationship exists between the other elements of the Enterprise Continuum.

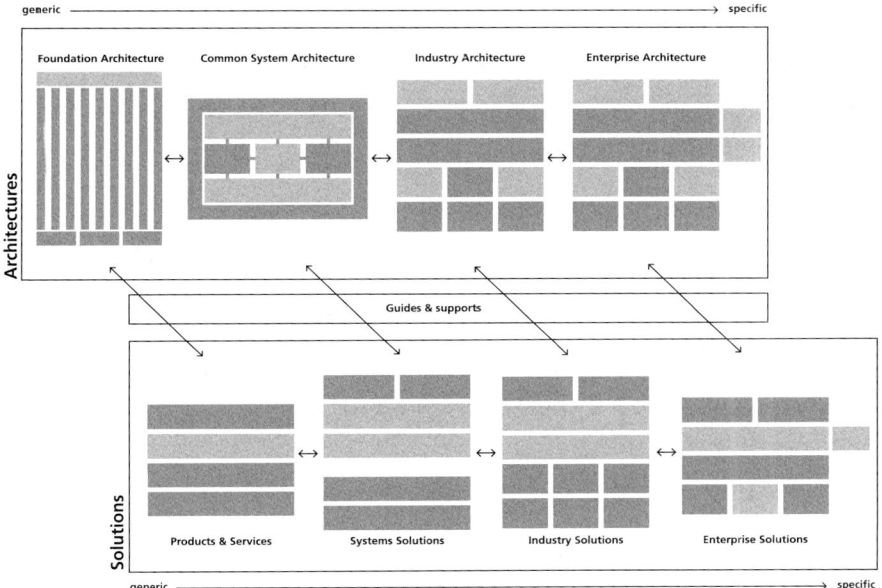

Figure 3.5 *The Enterprise Continuum*

3.3.1   The Foundation Architecture

The Foundation Architecture is an Architecture of generic services and functions that provides a foundation on which specific Architectures and architectural building blocks can be built. The Foundation Architecture includes the Technical Reference Model (TRM) and the Standards Information Base (SIB).

Technical Reference Model

The Technical Reference Model (TRM) provides a model and taxonomy of generic platform services. It defines the terminology and provides a coherent description of the components. It is meant to give the conceptual description of the Information System. It also provides a TRM graphic, which is a visual representation of the taxonomy and acts as an aid to understanding.

The TOGAF TRM emphasizes the aspect of interoperability, as well as that of portability and is platform-centric. The TRM gives a focus on the services and structure of the underlying platform that supports the use and re-use of applications. It concentrates on

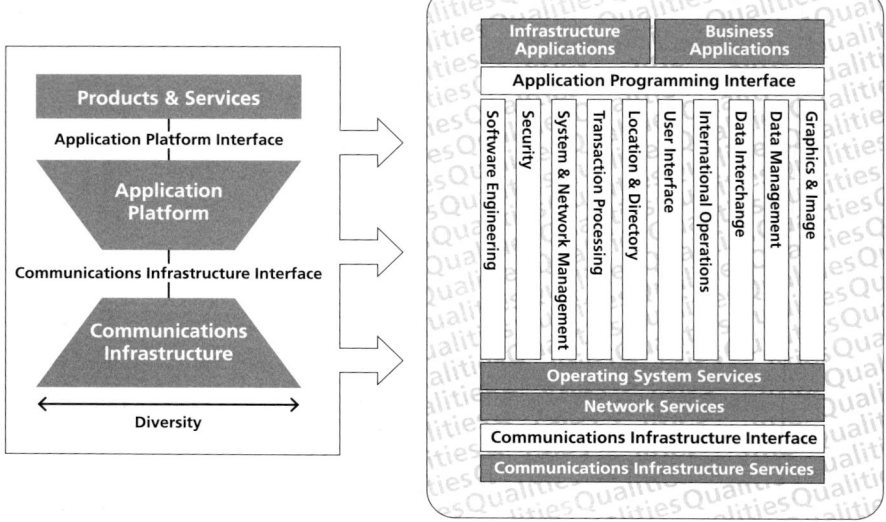

Figure 3.6 *The Technical Reference Model*

maximizing the diversity of the applications supported by the platform. It also maximizes the diversity of the supporting communication infrastructure.

Standards Information Base
The Standards Information Base (SIB) is a database of open industry standards that can be used to define the particular services and other components of an Enterprise-specific Architecture. The database is structured according to the taxonomy of the Technical Reference Model.

The SIB is a valuable source of information about standards that may be used to populate the Architecture during Architecture development. It can be used to define particular services and properties of components. It can also help to ensure that the procurement gives a clear statement of technical requirements with an assurance of conformance. The SIB can also be a source of information about relevant IT standards.

3.4   Resource Base

The Resource Base is a set of resources including guidelines, whitepapers, templates and background information to help the architect in the use of the ADM.

The Resource Base contains many lists of elements. An overview of subjects in the Resource Base can be found below:

Component	Short description
Architecture Board	Guidelines for establishing and operating an Enterprise Architecture Board to oversee the implementation of the strategy. This is a key element in a successful Architecture Governance Strategy.
Architecture Compliance	Guidelines and checklists for ensuring project compliance to Architecture. Ensuring the compliance of individual projects with the Enterprise Architecture is an essential aspect of Architecture Governance.
Architecture Contracts	Guidelines for defining and using Architecture Contracts. Architecture Contracts are the joint agreements between development partners and sponsors on the deliverables, quality, and fitness/for/purpose of Architecture.
Architecture Governance	A framework and guidelines for Architecture Governance. It describes arrangements for effective control of IT Architecture by Enterprise Management.
Architecture Maturity Models	A technique for evaluating and quantifying an organization's maturity in Enterprise Architecture.
Architecture Patterns	Guidelines on using Architecture Patterns.
Architecture Principles	Guidelines on developing Architecture Principles for the use and deployment of IT resources across the Enterprise, and gives a generic set of principles.
Architecture Skills Framework	Role, skill and experience norms for staff undertaking Enterprise Architecture work.
Architecture Views	Describes the role and taxonomy of Architecture Views and gives guidelines for developing viewpoints and views in Architecture Models.
Building Blocks Example	Explains the concept of building blocks and contains a fictional example illustrating use of building blocks in Architecture.
Business Process Domain Views	Presents a set of function views aligned with the business process structure of the Enterprise. A business process domain is a logical grouping of business systems dedicated to a common purpose.
Business Scenarios	Describes a method for deriving business requirements for Architecture and the implied technical requirements. A key factor in the success of Enterprise Architecture is the extent to which it is linked to business requirements and enables the Enterprise to achieve its business objectives.
Case Studies	Real-life examples showing TOGAF in use in a variety of situations.
Glossary	Definitions of terms essential to the understanding of TOGAF.

Component	Short description
Other Architectures / Frameworks	Brief description of several initiatives and their relationship to TOGAF.
Tools for Architecture Development	Generic evaluation criteria for Architecture tools and techniques that can be helpful in using TOGAF.
Zachman Framework Mapping	Provides a mapping of the TOGAF ADM to the Zachman Framework.

Three of these components are of specific interest within the context of this book, and can help to improve understanding of the Resource Base.

These are:
- Architecture Principles
- Architecture Viewpoints and Views
- Business Scenarios

3.4.1 Architecture Principles

Principles are general rules and guidelines that are intended to be enduring and seldom amended; they inform and support the way in which an organization sets about fulfilling its aims. Principles may be just one element in a structured set of ideas that collectively define and guide the organization from values through to actions and results. Principles form the basis for making all future IT decisions, and each architectural principle is related back to the business objectives and key Architecture drivers.

Architecture Principles are used to capture the fundamental truths about how the Enterprise will use and deploy IT resources and assets.

The Resource Base of TOGAF provides an example set of 20 defined principles which use a recommended format. This format provides a standard presentation for defining principles. The format contains the Name, Statement, Rationale, Implications and Dispensations for a given principle.

3.4.2 Architecture Viewpoints and Views

Architecture Views are representations of the overall Architecture, which are meaningful to one or more stakeholders. A set of Views will enable the Architecture to be communicated to and understood by all the stakeholders, and will enable them to verify that the system will address their requirements.

To understand the topic of viewpoints and views, it is important to have insight into the concepts that are central to it. TOGAF adopted and adapted these formal definitions from ANSI/IEEE Std 1471-2000:

System	A collection of components organized to accomplish a specific function or set of functions.
Architecture	The Architecture of a system is the system's fundamental organization, embodied in its components, their relationships to each other and to the environment, and the principles guiding its design and evolution.
Architecture Description	A collection of artifacts that documents Architecture. In TOGAF, Architecture Views are the key artifacts in an Architecture Description.
Stakeholders	People who have key roles in, or concerns about, the system: for example, as users, developers or managers. Different stakeholders with different roles in the system will have different concerns. Stakeholders can be individuals, teams or organizations (or classes thereof).
Concerns	The key interests that are crucially important to the stakeholders in the system. They determine the acceptability of the system. Concerns may pertain to any aspect of the system's functioning, development or operation, including considerations such as performance, reliability, security, distribution and resolvability.
View	A representation of a whole system from the perspective of a related set of concerns.
Viewpoint	Defines the perspective from which a view is taken. More specifically, a viewpoint defines: how to construct and use a view (by means of an appropriate schema or template); the information that should appear in the view; the modeling techniques for expressing and analyzing the information; and a rationale for these choices (e.g., by describing the purpose and intended audience of the view).

To address the concerns of the users TOGAF recommends developing Business Architecture Views. Technology Architecture Views are recommended to address the concerns of System and Software Engineers (Engineering views), Operators, Administrators and Managers (Operations views) and Acquirers (Acquirers' views).

3.4.3 Business Scenarios

Business Scenarios describe a method for deriving business requirements for Architecture. A Business Scenario is a complete description of the business challenges in business and architectural terms presented in text, diagrams and models. It ensures that the Architecture is based on a complete set of requirements, and that the business value of solving the problem and the relevance of potential solutions are clear. Using Business Scenarios can be helpful in getting the buy-in of business stakeholders.

In a Business Scenario a business process, an application, or set of applications, enabled by the suggested solution, is described. It also shows what the business and technology environment looks like and the desired outcome of proper execution. A good Business Scenario is representative for a significant market and enables the supply side to understand the value to the buy side of a developed solution. Therefore it needs to be SMART: Specific, Measurable, Actionable, Realistic and Time-bound.

CHAPTER 4

HOW: Frequently Asked Questions about using TOGAF

TOGAF has helped us to create
processes and awareness that
therefore save us money.
Bob Hennessy,
(Westpac Banking
Corporation, Australia)

4.1 Questions and Answers on TOGAF

> *Using a framework like TOGAF will enable you to design and manage multi-vendor Architecture solutions, and prevent you from being bound to any specific single vendor solution. The architecture development process will be more transparent and the solutions will be based on open systems and adapted to business needs.*
> **The Open Group; www.opengroup.org**

How can I use TOGAF?
TOGAF is published by The Open Group on its public website, and may be reproduced freely by any organization wishing to use it to develop an Information Systems Architecture within their organization.
As a member, after acquiring a commercial license, you can also develop your own tools, services or training courses based on TOGAF. By using The Open Group Certification services these can also be officially certified.

How much does TOGAF cost?
The Open Group operates as a not-for-profit consortium, committed to delivering greater business efficiency by bringing together buyers and suppliers of Information Systems.
TOGAF is a key part of The Open Group strategy for achieving this goal.

As an organization, The Open Group is keen for TOGAF to be adopted and used in practical Architecture projects. Members can adapt TOGAF to suit their own needs, and by feeding back their experiences into The Open Group consortium help to improve it. In order to facilitate this, The Open Group publishes TOGAF on its public web server, and allows and encourages its reproduction and use free-of-charge by any organization wishing to use it internally to develop an Information Systems Architecture.

By becoming a member, and actively participating in the development of TOGAF, the membership help to keep the cost of TOGAF at a minimum.

4.2   Questions and Answers on TOGAF Education and Certification

> *Certification provides assurance of conformance and shows vendors' confidence in, and commitment to, their products. It gives buyers confidence that products conform to standards and specifications, and are interoperable, and also that individuals have the required expertise and experience.*
> **The Open Group; www.opengroup.org**

What is TOGAF Certification and how can it benefit my organization?
TOGAF Certification is available for both individuals, i.e. Architects, and organizations. Individuals can become TOGAF certified by either demonstrating their knowledge by attending a training course or by passing an Open Group examination.

Organizations can have their products, like TOGAF tools or training courses, or their TOGAF-related services, certified.

The Certification program enables Enterprises to standardize on the open standard TOGAF. By certifying your staff and requiring TOGAF certified people, products and services from your partners and suppliers you can ensure that one common language and set of principles are used in your Architecture projects.

One of the main rationales behind The Open Group Certification programs is to simplify IT procurement, by producing open Product Standards reflecting requirements from the market, and to provide assurance of conformance and interoperability. This, of course, is in line with its vision of Boundaryless Information Flow™.

According to The Open Group, you can gain from certification in the following ways:

Main benefits to buyers of certified products:
* *get reliable assurance of conformance to standards and interoperability*
* *minimize need for conformance testing*

- *simplify bid analysis, and reduce procurement document complexity, cost and risk associated with procurement*

Main benefits to suppliers of certified systems:
- *show their commitment and demonstrate that they stand behind their products, which gives confidence to the buyers*
- *get access to a pool of major buyers who specify that the products they buy must be guaranteed to conform to the specifications*

What types of TOGAF Certification are there?
There are four types of TOGAF Certification, each, after complying with the requirements, entitling the use of its own logo:

LOGO	TYPE/Description
TOGAF 8 Certified	TOGAF Certification for Individuals; demonstrating knowledge of TOGAF by attending a certified training course or passing an Open Group examination.
TOGAF 8 Training	TOGAF Certification for Training Products conforming to the TOGAF Product Standard.
TOGAF 8 Professional Services	TOGAF Certification for Professional Services conforming to the TOGAF Product Standard.
TOGAF 8 Tool Support	TOGAF Certification for Tools conforming to the TOGAF Product Standard.

Certifications are published on the Certification Register, which is publicly accessible at the following URL:

https://www.opengroup.org/togaf/cert/

The Open Group also hosts two other Certification schemes, one for IT Architects (ITAC) and one for products.
- Under **the ITAC program**, practicing Enterprise and IT Architects can achieve the IT Architect Certification based on demonstrating substantial skills, experience and success in architecting solutions across the whole lifecycle.

The Open Group Certification Mark logo is a trademark of The Open Group and available for use under license only in connection with current certified products, services or individuals.

- Examples of **Certified products** include:
  - *COE*
  - *CORBA®*
  - *LDAP*
  - *NASPL*
  - *POSIX®*
  - *SIF*
  - *TOGAF^{TM}*
  - *UNIX®*
  - *WAP*

What is the main difference between TOGAF and ITAC Certification?

The Open Group defines the two Certification schemes as follows:

- The IT Architect Certification program is agnostic about methods and is concerned instead with an architect's skills and experience - their ability to deliver business value to their clients.
- TOGAF is one of the methods used in the IT Architecture domain. TOGAF Certification confirms an individual's knowledge of the TOGAF Architecture Development Method (ADM) and the TOGAF body of knowledge.

Where can I get TOGAF education?

A good starting point is the *'TOGAF Showcase'* page on The Open Group website. It can be found at the following URL: http://www.opengroup.org/togaf/cert/showcase/ On this web page certified training courses, tools and providers of services that are TOGAF certified are featured.

CHAPTER 5

Why Shell Oil chose TOGAF: A Case Study

'Knowledge is an important asset for Shell' says Johan Krebbers, one of their main Enterprise Architects. The Shell Oil Company uses a lot of Information Systems to find, explore and produce oil, in order to make products out of it to sell to their customers. To find new sources of oil before others do, and to develop means to explore this oil at lower cost than others, has become a complex engineering business. To achieve this Shell is increasingly working together with partners.

Johan Krebbers continues: 'Our scenarios tell us that we are tending to operate in an open world, where organizations have to work together in constantly changing partnerships in order to stay successful. The right information at the right time is a key factor in this development; we not only have to be good in producing the right information, we need to know were it is and how to access it at the right time.'

The entire Shell Oil Company, worldwide, must work together and exchange its knowledge in order to be successful in its core business; meaning that it has to extract more oil out of the earth and make a profit selling that oil and its derivatives. 'We call it the upstream and the downstream business, and we are leading in the way we do our business', Mr Krebbers explains. The upstream and downstream businesses are, in fact, the business drivers that stimulate the development of applications and IT infrastructures. When new IT capabilities can support these drivers they will be put on the management agenda. The primary goal is to achieve the best possible alignment between Business and IT.

Enterprise Architecture can be used to support this business process. In Shell the Enterprise Architecture is divided into three layers: Business, Applications and Technology. Architecture is used to extract the principles from the business drivers and translate them into requirements for Applications and Technology. Based on these principles, Architecture is used to describe all services that are delivered to the Shell organizations that use them. The transformation from the 'as is' to the 'desired' state are described in 'roadmaps'. To further help the user organizations to use the services involved effectively, patterns that describe how to use the services or products are developed. All principles involved are developed and agreed in close co-operation with the business."

In order to get all the involved architects, from Shell or from its partners, to develop Enterprise Architecture in the same way, and to let them all speak the same language, Shell has developed a toolset based on TOGAF.

'With TOGAF we can be sure that all parties involved speak the same language, use the same open method and can be certified independently. And furthermore, with TOGAF, we can review our own Enterprise Architecture globally based on the same standard'

Johan Krebbers
Group IT Architect, Shell I.T. International

Annex A: Terminology and Acronyms

*"The difference between the almost
right word and the right word is like
the difference between the lightning
bug and the lightning."*
Mark Twain

ADM
Architecture Development Method.

ANSI
American National Standards Institute.

API
Application Program Interface (API)
The interface, or set of functions, between
the Application Software and the Application
Platform. The most common means by which
a software programmer invokes other software
functions.

Application Software
Software entities which have a specific business
purpose.

Architecture
Architecture has two meanings depending upon
its contextual usage:
- a formal description of a system, or a detailed
  plan of the system at component level to guide
  its implementation
- the structure of components, their inter-
  relationships, and the principles and guidelines
  governing their design and evolution over time

Architecture Continuum
A part of the Enterprise Continuum. The
Architecture Continuum provides a repository
for architectural elements with increasing detail
and specialization. This Continuum begins with
foundational definitions like reference models,
core strategies and basic building blocks. From

there it spans to Industry Architectures and all the way to an organization's specific Architecture.

Architecture Framework	A tool for assisting in the production of organization-specific Architectures. An Architecture framework consists of a Technical Reference Model (TRM), a method for Architecture development, and a list of component standards, specifications, products and their inter-relationships, which can be used to build up Architectures.
Architecture View	A perspective from which an Architecture may be viewed in order to ensure that a specific topic is considered in a coherent manner, eg security.
Baseline	A specification or product that has been formally reviewed and agreed upon, that thereafter serves as the basis for further development and that can be changed only through formal change control procedures, or a type of procedure such as configuration management.
Baseline Architecture	The existing system Architecture before entering a cycle of Architecture review and redesign.
Business System	Hardware, software, policy statements, procedures and people which together implement a business function.
Client	An application component which requests services from a server.
CoBiT	Control OBjectives for Information and related Technology.
Communications System	A set of assets (transmission media, switching nodes, interfaces and control devices) that will establish linkage between users and devices.

Configuration direction Management	A discipline applying technical and administrative and surveillance to: • identify and document the functional and physical characteristics of a configuration item • control changes to those characteristics • record and report changes to processing and implementation status
Connectivity Service	A service area of the External Environment entity of the Technical Reference Model (TRM) that provides end-to-end connectivity for communications through three transport levels (global, regional and local). It provides general and application-specific services to platform end devices.
CORBA	Common Object Request Broker Architecture.
Data Dictionary	A specialized type of database containing metadata, which is managed by a data dictionary system; a repository of information describing the characteristics of data used to design, monitor, document, protect and control data in Information Systems and databases; an application of data dictionary systems.
Database Architecture	The logical view of the data models, data standards and data structure. It includes a definition of the physical databases for the Information System, their performance requirements and their geographical distribution.
Data Element	A basic unit of information having a meaning and that may have subcategories (data items) of distinct units and values.
Database	Structured or organized collection of information, which may be accessed by the computer.

Data Interchange Service — A service of the Platform entity of the Technical Reference Model (TRM) that provides specialized support for the interchange of data between applications on the same or different platforms.

Data Management Service — A service of the Platform entity of the Technical Reference Model (TRM) that provides support for the management, storage, access and manipulation of data in a database.

DBMS — Database Management System -computer application program that accesses or manipulates the database.

DCE — Distributed Computing Environment.

DDL — Data Definition Language.

Directory Service — Part of the network services of the Application Platform entity of the Technical Reference Model (TRM) that provides locator services that are restricted to finding the location of a service, location of data, or translation of a common name into a network-specific address. It is analogous to telephone books and supports distributed directory implementations.

DISA — US Department of Defense Information Systems Agency.

Distributed Database — A database that is not stored in a central location, but is dispersed over a network of interconnected computers.
A database under the overall control of a central Database Management System (DBMS) but whose storage devices are not all attached to the same processor.
A database that is physically located in two or more distinct locations.

DMF	Data Management Facility.
ECMA	European Computer Manufacturers Association.
EDI	Electronic Data Interchange.
EEI	External Environment Interface.
End User	Person who ultimately uses the computer application or output.
Enterprise	The highest level in an organization; includes all missions and functions.
Enterprise Continuum	Comprises two complementary concepts: the Architecture Continuum and the Solutions Continuum. Together, these are a range of definitions with increasing specificity, from foundational definitions and agreed Enterprise strategies, all the way to Architectures and implementations in specific organizations. Such co-existence of abstraction and concreteness in an Enterprise can be a real source of confusion. The Enterprise Continuum also doubles as a powerful tool to turn confusion and resulting conflicts into progress.
Enterprise Model	A high-level model of an organization's mission, function and information Architecture. The model consists of a function model and a data model.
ERP	Enterprise Resource Planning.
ES	End System.
Expand	Ability to resize objects to produce better organization of on-screen material, usually a graphic or a window.

External Environment	The interface that supports information transfer between
Interface (EEI)	the Application Platform and the External environment.
File	Any specifically identified collection of information stored in the computer.
FIPS	Federal Information Processing Standard.
FORTRAN	FORmula TRANslator; a high-level computer language used extensively in scientific and engineering applications.
FTAM	File Transfer, Access, and Management.
Function	A useful capability provided by one or more components of a system.
GNMP	Government Network Management Profile.
GOSIP	Government Open System Interconnection Profile.
GSS	General Security Service.
GUI	Graphical User Interface.
Hardware	Physical equipment, as opposed to programs, procedures, rules and associated documentation. Contrast with software.
Human Computer Interface (HCI)	Human Computer Interface hardware and soft ware, allowing information exchange between the user and the computer.

IEC	The International Electro Technical Commission; the international standards body which is responsible for electrical standards.
IEEE	Institute of Electrical and Electronic Engineers.
III	Integrated Information Infrastructure.
III-RM	Integrated Information Infrastructure Reference Model.
Information	Any communication or representation of knowledge such as facts, data or opinions, in any medium or form, including textual, numerical, graphic, cartographic, narrative or audio-visual forms.
Information Domain	A set of commonly and unambiguously labelled information objects, with a common security policy that defines the protections to be afforded the objects by authorized users and information management systems.
Information System	The computer-based portion of a business system.
Information Technology (IT)	The technology included in hardware and software used for information, regardless of the technology involved, whether computers, communications, micro graphics or others.
Interface	Interconnection and inter-relationships between two devices, two applications, or the user and an application or device.
Interoperability	The ability of two or more systems or components to exchange and use information.
	The ability of systems to provide and receive services from other systems and to use the

	services so interchanged to enable them to operate effectively together.
IS	Information System.
ISA	Information Systems Architecture.
ISO	International Standards Organization.
IT	Information Technology.
ITIL	Information Technology Infrastructure Library.
JTC1	A Joint Technical Committee established by ISO and IEC to take responsibility for their shared interests in IT standardization.
LAN	Local Area Network.
Lifecycle	The period of time that begins when a system is conceived and ends when the system is no longer available for use.
MAN	Metropolitan Area Network.
Metaview (also known constructing and as a Viewpoint)	A specification of the conventions for using a view. A metaview acts as a pattern or template of the view, from which to develop individual views. A metaview establishes the purposes and audience for a view, the ways in which the view is documented (e.g. for visual modelling), and the ways in which it is used (e.g. for analysis).
MIS	Management Information Systems.
MLS	Multi-Level Security.
MTA	Message Transfer Agent.

Multimedia Service	A service of the Technical Reference Model (TRM) that provides the capability to manipulate and manage information products consisting of text, graphics, images, video and audio.
NIST	US National Institute of Standards and Technology.
NLSP	Network Layer Security Protocol.
ODA	Office Document Architecture.
ODIF	Office Document Interchange Format.
OECD	Organization for Economic Co-operation and Development.
OODBMS	Object-Oriented Database Management System.
Open Specifications	Public specifications that are maintained by an open, public consensus process to accommodate new technologies over time and that are consistent with international standards.
Open System	A system that implements sufficient open specifications for interfaces, services and supporting formats to enable properly engineered Application Software: • to be ported with minimal changes across a wide range of systems • to interoperate with other applications on local and remote systems • to interact with users in a style that facilitates user portability
Open Systems Environment (OSE)	The comprehensive set of interfaces, services and supporting formats, plus user aspects for interoperability or for portability of applications, data, or people, as specified by IT standards and profiles.

Operating System Service	A core service of the Application Platform entity of the Technical Reference Model (TRM) that is needed to operate and administer the Application Platform and provide an interface between the Application Software and the Platform (e.g. file management, input/output, print spoolers).
ORB	Object Request Broker.
OS	Operating System.
OSE	Open System Environment.
OSI	Open Systems Interconnection.
PEX	PHIGS Extension to X Windows.
PHIGS	Programmer's Hierarchical Interactive Graphics System.
Portability	The ease with which a system or component can be transferred from one hardware or software environment to another. A quality metric that can be used to measure the relative effort to transport the software for use in another environment or to convert software for use in another operating environment, hardware configuration or software system environment. The ease with which a system, component, data or user can be transferred from one hardware or software environment to another.
POSIX	Portable Operating System Interface (for Computer Environments).
Profile	A set of one or more base standards and, where applicable, the identification of those classes, subsets, options, and parameters of those base standards, necessary for accomplishing a particular function.

Profiling	Selecting standards for a particular application.
RAS	Remote Access Services.
RDA	Remote Database Access.
RDBMS	Relational Database Management System.
Repository	A system that manages all of the data of an Enterprise, including data and process models and other Enterprise information. Hence, the data in a repository is much more extensive than that in a data dictionary, which generally defines only the data making up a database.
RM	Reference Model.
Scalability	The ability to use the same Application Software on many different classes of hardware / software platforms from PCs to super-computers (extends the portability concept). The capability to grow to accommodate increased workloads.
Security	Services which protect data, ensuring its confidentiality, availability and integrity.
SGML	Standard Generalized Markup Language.
SIB	Standards Information Base.
SMAP	Security Management Application Process.
SMTP	Simple Mail Transfer Protocol.
SNA	System Network Architecture.
SNMP	Simple Network Management Protocol.

Solutions Continuum	A part of the Enterprise Continuum. The Solutions Continuum contains implementations of the corresponding definitions in the Architecture Continuum. In this way it becomes a repository of reusable solutions for future implementation efforts.
SQL	Structured Query Language.
System	A collection of components organized to accomplish a specific function or set of functions (taken from Draft Recommended Practice for Architectural Description IEEE P1471/D5.2).
System and Network Management Service	A cross-category service of the Application Platform entity of the Technical Reference Model (TRM) that provides for the administration of the overall Information System. These services include the management of information, processors, networks, configurations, accounting and performance.
System Stakeholder	An individual, team or organization (or classes thereof) with interests in, or concerns relative to, a system (taken from ANSI/IEEE Std 1471-2000).
TAFIM	Technical Architecture Framework for Information Management.
Target Architecture	Depicts the configuration of the target Information System.
Taxonomy of Architecture Views	The organized collection of all views pertinent to an Architecture.
TCP/IP	Transmission Control Protocol/Internet Protocol.

TCSEC	Trusted Computer System Evaluation Criteria.
Technical Reference Model	A structure which allows the components of an Information System to be described in a consistent manner.
TFA	Transparent File Access.
TLSP	Transport Layer Security Protocol.
TNI	Trusted Network Interpretation.
TP	Transaction Processing.
Transaction	Interaction between a user and a computer in which the user inputs a command to receive a specific result from the computer.
Transaction Sequence	Order of transactions required to accomplish the desired results.
TRM	Technical Reference Model.
TSIG	Trusted Systems Interoperability Group.
UIDL	User Interface Definition Language.
UIMS	User Interface Management System.
UISRM	User Interface System Reference Model.
User	Any person, organization, or functional unit that uses the services of an information processing system. In a conceptual schema language, any person or any thing that may issue or receive commands and messages to or from the Information System.

User Interface Service	A service of the Application Platform entity of the Technical Reference Model (TRM) that supports direct human-machine interaction by controlling the environment in which users interact with applications.
View	A representation of a whole system from the perspective of a related set of concerns.
Viewpoint (also known as a Metaview)	A specification of the conventions for constructing and using a view. A metaview acts as a pattern or template of the view, from which to develop individual views. A metaview establishes the purposes and audience for a view, the ways in which the view is documented (e.g. for visual modelling) and the ways in which it is used (e.g. for analysis).
WAN	Wide Area Network.

Annex B: Recommended Reading and Bibliography

The Boundaryless Organization: Breaking the Chains of Organizational Structure (The Jossey-Bass Management Series) by Ronald N. Ashkenas (Author), Dave Ulrich (Author),C. K. Prahalad (Author), Toad Jick (Author)

- **Publisher:** Jossey-Bass; 1st ed edition (September 1995)
- **Language:** English
- **ISBN-13:** 978-0787901134

Index